The Gentle People

A PORTRAIT OF THE AMISH

The Gentle People

A PORTRAIT OF THE AMISH

JAMES A. WARNER • DONALD DENLINGER

THE GENTLE PEOPLE: A Portrait of the Amish

A MIDDLE ATLANTIC PRESS BOOK

First Middle Atlantic Press printing, August 1985

ISBN: 0-912608-23-4 (hardcover)
0-912608-27-7 (Trade Paper)

The Middle Atlantic Press, Inc.
848 Church Street
Wilmington, Delaware 19899

Printed in Spain by Printer I.G.S.A.
Barcelona D.L.B. 18093-1985

The Gentle People

A PORTRAIT OF THE AMISH

"DEDICATED TO"

George Samos: Representative of Photographic Society of America, for his help in proof editing,

and

Edwin Smith, Jr.: Photographic consultant for his assistance in making this book possible.

Love not the world, neither the
things that are in the world,
If any man love the world, the
love of the Father is not in him.

I John 2:15

Wherefore come out from among them,
and be ye separate, saith the Lord,
and touch not the unclean thing, and
I will receive you.

II Cor. 6:17

. . . . they are like grass which
groweth up.
In the morning it flourisheth,
and groweth up: in the evening
it is cut down, and withereth.
Psalm 90:6, 7

The Gentle People

Amidst our highly industrialized, mechanized and scientific society in which we live, there exists a group of people who have chosen to live within a fixed, and almost static social structure. These people call themselves Amish. Based upon the faith and customs of their fore-fathers, the Amish place a premium on stability rather than change or advancement. Thus they eliminate fads, social status, and worldly stresses and allurements. Their wants are their needs, and their needs are their everyday basic requirements.

Their mode of transportation is the horse-drawn carriage. Next year's model will have the same style as last year's model. If they take care of the carriage they have after marriage, it will probably last them till death.

Amish clothing styles are dictated by the ORDNUNG (code of church discipline). Thus styles never change, nor do the Amish dare to change even the up or down of their hem lines. Most of their clothing is hand made by the women, who buy remnants and broadcloth by the yard for this purpose. Making this clothing keeps the women busy during the long cold winter evenings.

Men's wear consists of black suits with no buttons, just hooks and eyes. The Amish, who are pacifists, are opposed to buttons since they have a military origin. Their shirts can be colored, but designs or prints are not allowed. Neckties and bowties are taboo. A broad rimmed straw hat is worn in the summer, and a black felt hat in winter, with no less than a three inch rim.

Married women wear black bonnets and black or dark colored full length dresses. Unmarried women wear white aprons, changing to black aprons after marriage, which they wear until death. Their white mesh prayer bonnets must be worn at all times.

The Amish need not reach beyond their immediate society to satisfy their major social, physical, spiritual or emotional needs. The pure basics of life have given them a solidarity which makes them virtually self-sufficient in their community.

Old age pensions, social security, and insurance are not sanctioned because their people rally around one in need, or in an emergency. They have a profound respect for one another and their God, which is the catalyst for their existence in our contemporary world.

Their history of persecution in the old world, as graphically portrayed in Martyrs' Mirror, gave them ties and utter dependence in each other. The extreme persecution also gave them a reluctance to change, and a distrust of those outside their own.

The Amish broke away from the Mennonites in the late 17th century not because of the hard persecution from the state church, but because of the controversy over the MEIDUNG (or shunning of the excommunicated).

The early Mennonites and Menno Simmons of Holland believed this doctrine would assure the purity of the Mennonite Church.

The split came from the literal concept of MEIDUNG, led by Jacob Ammon who thought I Cor. 5:11 which states "If any man that is called a railer or a drunkard or an extortioner, with such a one not to eat," meant a tangible or physical meal.

The Mennonites started taking a more liberal view in the late 17th century saying Christ ate with Publicans and sinners in Gallilee but did not take communion with them, thus shunning the excommunicated is a spiritual application only.

Because of this view Jacob Ammon became sectarian and declared the Mennonites as apostate and liberals.

Therefore in the early 1720's they migrated to Pennsylvania from Switzerland and found an abundance of land for their community farms, and an unmolested freedom to worship as a segregated clan.

Almost 250 years have passed but Amish customs, methods of transportation, farming and entertainment have changed very little.

But the fruit of the Spirit is
love, joy, peace, long suffering,
gentleness, goodness, faith,
meekness, temperance:

Gal. 5:24

Thou wilt keep him in perfect peace, whose mind is stayed on thee: because he trusteth in thee.

Isaiah 26:3

My soul, wait thou only upon God:
for my expectation is from him.

Psalm 62:5

The wind bloweth where it listeth,
and thou hearest the sound there-
of, but canst not tell whence it
cometh, and whither it goeth:

John 3:8

And be not conformed to this world: but be ye transformed by the renewing of your mind. . . .

Romans 12:2

Amish Home Foundations

The home is the pulse of Amish life. It is the Alpha and Omega (the beginning and the ending) of their lives, and the few God-given years between are a symphony of homespun learning and hard work, mixed with impromptu fun and frolic. The children learn to speak Pennsylvania Dutch at home. Amish church services are held in their homes. Get-togethers and group singings take place in their homes. Courtship and marriage take place in their home. Even the viewings and funeral services for the departed are held at home.

Amish houses are very plain and modest and usually have sprawling wings or additions built onto the main house, called "Grossdawdy House." The large homestead farm is passed down from generation to generation. Sometimes, three or four generations may live in one house at a time.

Simplicity and cleanliness is the order of their homes. The Pennsylvania Amish seem to prefer brick or wood frame houses, painted grey or white, with contrasting green or dark grey window frames. Picket fences, tree trunks, and old walls around the yard are always kept whitewashed to reflect cleanliness. To the Amish, "cleanliness is next to Godliness."

Inside the house, the lack of window curtains and walls void of pictures are hardly noticed because your attention is captured by the vivid colored rugs, pillows, afghans, quilts, and glassware strategically placed. It is the utility of these brightly colored decorations that makes them acceptable at the same time eliminating the need for pictures and curtains.

Furniture is passed down from generation to generation, yet is never considered antique. Most of the furniture is varnished natural wood, and is hand made by Amish cabinet makers.

Contrasted with our modern, all-electric kitchen is the Amish kitchen. This is huge in size, and features a large old stove almost in the center, with an eight-board family table a few yards away. Most of the activity centers around the polished black stove, from the baking of bread, pies, and succulent meals, to the heating of water for baths, and oh yes, the feet warming in the oven after the chores in sub-zero weather. This large coal or wood burning range is also the only heat source for the large kitchen and possibly the room directly above.

The lack of radio, television, record players, and electricity virtually cuts the Amish off from the stresses, strains, and allurements of the outside world. The long winter evenings are spent around the kitchen range as the father of the house reads the old German Bible, Mom sews or braids rugs, and the children play checkers or study. The steady purring of the gas lantern, the rhythmic tic of the mantle clock, and an occasional snap or crackling of the fire in the range are the only sounds that break the peace and quietness of the evenings.

By eight-thirty or nine, the children, one by one, take a lantern to visit the small building behind the woodshed, then disappear up to their room without much coaxing. They know that at five o'clock in the morning there will come a firm call to help with the morning chores and they had better obey.

The persistent urgency of the rooster's crowing almost eliminates the need for an alarm clock. You would guess the sun couldn't rise without his beckoning call. Since Amish bedrooms have no heat, it doesn't take long for the children to dress in the fading moonlight. So, the typical Amish day begins. By seven thirty the numerous morning chores are completed. A healthy appetite ensues which demands a well rounded, full course breakfast before "dressing around" and hurrying off to school.

When the children become teen-agers, especially in large families, the older boys are hired out as laborers and carpenter's helpers, while the girls hire out as cleaning maids. All the wages they earn are turned over to their parents until they become eighteen. Then, they are usually allowed to keep half of their weekly wages until they marry. This financial jurisdiction seems almost dictatorial. However, it is a very adhesive factor, fundamental in holding the young people in the Amish faith.

If an Amish young man "goes gay," he is shunned by the church. He is also shunned by his family and cannot eat at the same table. His father is also relieved of the obligation in providing a farm for that son.

In the case of a daughter "going gay," she relinquishes her rights to Haush-dier, or the furnishings for her new house, which the bride's father always provides. Hence, any aspirations to leave the Amish society are dispelled when they consider the consequences.

The young folks are raised so carefully within the Amish family and society that they never feel secure outside of it.

A question might arise in your mind as to what can be done if a member of the faith breaks away and then decides to return. The following true anecdote will answer this question.

A young Amish fellow had a craving for the outside world and the many things it had to offer. Not being married, he broke away and joined the US Air Force. He completed his schooling and climbed the ranks to fly in supersonic jets. This was great and fascinating until his honorable discharge cast him back into civilian life. Here, a man without a home, loneliness caught up with him.

His memories of a childhood sweetheart haunted him till he returned to see what became of her. She was still a maidal (unmarried), but still of the old order Amish, which forbad his trespassing on her farm. However, outside rendezvous soon rekindled their love. They went to the Bishop, confessed and repented to the church which received them back. The lad is now an old order Amishman who went from supersonic jet speeds back to the slow pace of a horse and buggy.

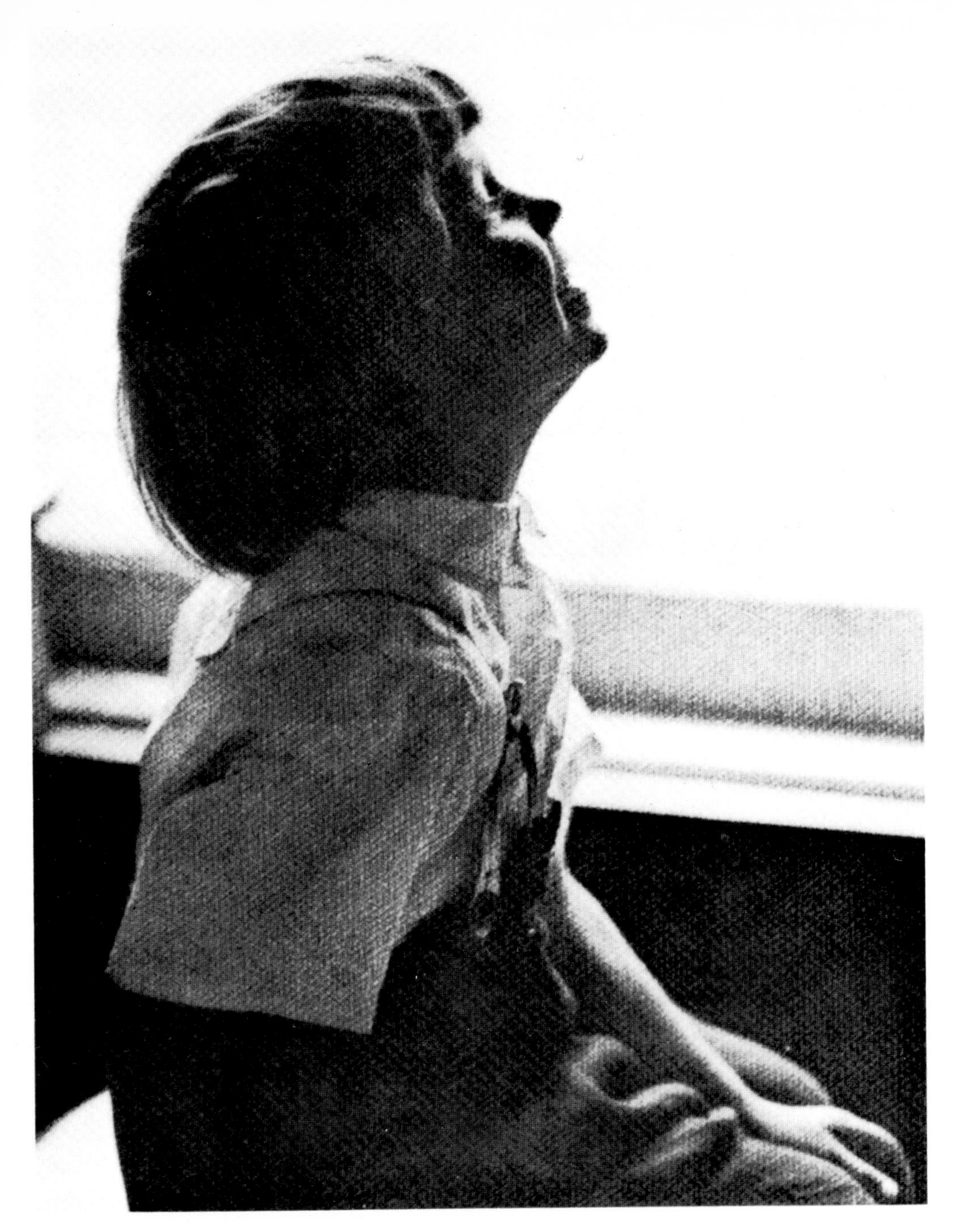

Rejoice, O young man, in thy youth; and let thy heart cheer thee in the days of thy youth, and walk in the ways of thine heart, and in the sight of thine eyes.
Ecclesiates 11:9

Study to show thyself approved unto God, a workman that needeth not to be ashamed, rightly dividing the word of truth.

II Timothy 2:15

Whatsoever thy hand findeth to do, do it with thy might.

Ecclesiastes 9:10

He giveth power to the faint:
and to them that have no might
he increaseth strength.

. . . they that wait upon the Lord
shall renew their strength: they
shall mount up with wings as
eagles: they shall run, and not
be weary: and they shall walk,
and not faint.

Isaiah 40:31

Let the children first show piety
at home, and to requite their
parents; for that is good and
acceptable before God.

I Timothy 5:4

The Lord is my strength and my shield; my heart trusted in him, and I am helped: therefore my heart greatly rejoiceth: and with my song will I praise him.

Psalm 28:7

Slothfulness casteth into a deep sleep; and an idle soul shall suffer hunger.

Proverbs 19:15

. . . and I shall be clean: wash me,
and I shall be whiter than snow.

Psalms 51:7

Peace I leave with you, my peace I give unto you: not as the world giveth, give I unto you. Let not your heart be troubled, neither let it be afraid.

John 14:27

Little Red School House

Nostalgic red one-room school houses, similar to those our fore-fathers attended, are still evident around the Amish country side. Each school is responsible for the children within a four-mile radius so that no child has to walk more than two miles to school. The children take advantage of every shortcut, crossing fields and meadows, where, in winter every weed is dressed in sparkling icy grandeur, and where the occasional flurry of a rabbit or pheasant breaks up the monotony of the long hike. By the time they have climbed the last fence into the school yard, the tolling of the quaint rusty bell in the wooden belfry is heard, giving late-comers just enough time to hang their wraps on the pegs and rush to their seats for roll call and the eight o'clock devotions. The teacher will then read some verses from the German Bible (Martin Luther's translation), followed by the Lord's Prayer in German.

Teaching four subjects in one room, to eight grades consisting of approximately forty to fifty pupils, poses a complex problem demanding unusual teaching strategy and technique. The first graders know little if any English, and the fourth through eighth graders must be taught Hi-German since their Bibles and sermons are not written in the Pennsylvania Dutch dialect.

The most effective approach used is to give the older students, who meet certain grade standards, the privilege of helping the first and second graders learn English. Another effective technique is to concentrate on one or two subjects a day. This means everyone is learning English on Monday, arithmetic on Tuesday, penmanship on Wednesday, and so on. The eight grades seem to absorb more readily when subjects are segregated this way.

When the teacher pulls the rope for the noon lunch bell, she is usually caught in a stampede as the youngsters make a dash for their brightly colored lunch buckets. Their lunches are usually eaten in five-minutes time so they can have the other twenty-five minutes for playing baseball, drop-the-hankie, or hop-scotch.

Each morning and afternoon session is divided into two parts by fifteen minute recesses, and dismissal takes place at 3:30 P.M. Ironically, the stampede that takes place at lunch time is not repeated at dismissal. In fact, the children joke and frolic, and may even take the longer way home. They know that chores are waiting when they get home from school.

When a child receives eight years of basic education, or completes the eighth grade with strong emphasis on the three R's (reading, writing, and arithmetic), he is considered to have the educational background to lead a normal life in the Amish society. To get a high school education is considered unnecessary and worldly. Instead of receiving a high school education, the teen-aged girl is taught the basics of home-making, while the teen-aged boy is being instructed in the essentials of prosperous farming. By the time he reaches seventeen or eighteen years, he has the basics of animal husbandry, crop rotation, and farm finances equivalent to a college agricultural student.

During the past several decades, state education departments have made progress in getting the Amish to utilize the public schools, eliminating most of the one-room schools. Consequently, very few are still operated under public funding. Those that are still operating are staffed with a state-certified non-Amish teacher, although all the students are Amish. The continuing of these one-room schools is the result of pressure brought upon local school boards by Amish families and Bishops.

The encroachment of the state upon the Amish philosophy of education has resulted in an Amish parochial school program. The state of Pennsylvania has allowed Amish families to operate and staff their own schools. When the state closes one of the schools, it is sold at public auction and the Amish families of the surrounding district purchase it. However, the limited number of existing buildings purchased from the state are not sufficient to meet the pressing demands of the large families. Thus, farmers relinquish small parcels of their land upon which one-room schools are built.

Operation of these schools is patterned after methods used several decades ago. They are staffed by teachers who have had no more than an eighth grade education, and are usually maiden ladies of the Amish sect, never men.

An Amish school-teacher is given the highest esteem by the parents. She is given full reign in disciplinary matters and, more often than not, the older boys get the "Amish board of education on their seat of learning."

"Spare the rod and spoil the child" is the Amish philosophy in the training of children.

Let no man despise thy youth: but be thou an example of the believers in word, in conversation, in charity, in spirit, in faith, in purity.
I Tim. 4:12

Train up a child in the way he should go: and when he is old, he will not depart from it.

Proverbs 22:6

Wisdom is the principal thing:
therefore get wisdom: and with
all thy getting get understanding.

Prov. 4:7

Bb Cc Dd Ee Ff Gg Hh

For I will pour water upon him
that is thirsty, and floods upon
the dry ground: I will pour my
spirit upon thy seed, and my
blessing upon thine offspring:

Isaiah 44:3

For the wisdom of this world is
foolishness with God. For it is
written, He taketh the wise in
their own craftiness.

I Corinthians 3:19

For lo, the winter is past,
the rain is over and gone,
the flowers appear on the earth:
the time of the singing of birds is
come, and the voice of the turtle
dove is heard in our land:

Song of Sol. 2:11, 12

The Lord is my shepherd; I shall not want. He maketh me to lie down in green pastures: He leadeth me beside the still waters.

Psalms 23:1-2

A fountain of gardens, a well of living waters, and streams from Lebanon.

Song of Solomon 4:15

Whoso findeth a wife,
findeth a good thing, and
obtaineth favour of the Lord.
Proverbs 18:22

Entertainment

From everything that has been said about the Amish way of life, one would assume that these gentle people do nothing but work their years away. Naturally, this is not so as the Amish are just as much interested in fun and entertainment as any one else. However, their forms of entertainment differ from those of the non-Amish. Their activities are less boisterous and not as flamboyant as those in which the non-Amish participate. Their entertainment usually involves doing something constructive with their friends and neighbors, while at the same time they are sharing their home and bread. The youngsters' forms of entertainment, however, are quite different.

Youngsters tease and frolic like playful kittens. Their toys are usually home-made dolls or wooden wagons, without the frills and elaborate reality of the toys other children use. In their adolescent years, almost all their play takes place within segregated groups of either boys or girls; each group trying to outsmart the other with some practical joke.

With the girls, playing dolls or hide the thimble are favorite games, but hopscotch, rope-skipping, or picking flowers are more favored on bright summer days when they can play outside.

The adolescent boys, bursting with energy, are like young billy goats. What they cannot get into they climb up, over, around or under. They need no formal games, and only a limited amount of props to expend their energy and imagination. They are frequently found running through the stables and barn yard pulling their toy wagon with some string or bailing twine held in their mouth, like Pop's horse and buggy. Tiring of this after several hours, they may head for the babbling brook in the meadow with a piece of string, a fish hook and a tree branch for a pole. Being full of life, their patience doesn't afford waiting for the fish to bite. They will roll up their pant legs and go wading, or else chase a fluttering butterfly to the farthest corner of the farm.

As they become of school age and on up to teenagers, a tendency towards group games and organized competition prevails. During school recess, groups of playmates play such games as fox and geese, bag tag, kick the can, and baseball, games they can play for hours on end without tiring. During their teenage years, the girls start to enjoy needle work, quilting and rug braiding, and if they can't sew their own clothes by then they "chust ain't had the right bringing up."

The young fellows have less and less time for play as they assume more of the chores and responsibilities around the farm. However, they are usually given their own calf or hog, or sometimes a pony to raise and take pride in.

Checkers and chess are popular games, but cards are frowned upon as a wholesome game. Sledding and ice-skating are enjoyed immensely, and when the old mill stream is frozen, there may be several games of ice hockey going on at the same time. After dark, when the evening chores are completed, lanterns are lit and an ice-skating marathon on the frozen streams under the stars, ensues. If there is snow on the ground, Old Dobbin is hitched to the sleigh for a ride in the cold, clear, refreshing air.

Young fellows who have been given their first team of horses enjoy studding the harnesses with extra silver buttons and shine their carriages for a Sunday afternoon ride past a favorite girl's farm or to go to a neighboring farm for a singing.

Several hundred young people may congregate in a barn for the singing. Couples sit in one section of the barn. Maidals sit on benches in another section while the boys sit on bales and hay mows. Singing is a source of inspirational integration of their deepest emotional spirit. This is evident in both the content of their music and in the manner of singing. Their Ashbund (hymnal), derived from the Gregorian chants of Southern Germany, was first published in 1564. This most unusual 812 page song book contains only 140 songs and not a note of music or scale. The Amish vorsinger (song leader) sets the pitch and sings the first syllable of each line. The rest of the congregation sense the succeeding notes, and in unison, join in a slow entrancing chant. The tempo of the singing is stepped up as they sing the contemporary Protestant type songs from the Lieder Saumlunger. Musical instruments for hymns are not allowed because "God gave us voices to praise him," and instruments break up the worshipful atmosphere of the old hymns.

After the singing is finished and the older parents have departed, the group pair off and a square dance starts. Some of the boys bring a fiddle, a guitar, and possibly several mouth organs and form an impromptu band to play such tunes as Turkey in the Straw, Six-Handed Reel, O-H-I-O, Skip To My Lou, and many others. The old order Amish prohibit dancing but do not consider these folk games as dances, in the strict sense of the word.

In the fall of the year in Lancaster County, corn husking bees were common. Each couple would take a corn shock and try to finish theirs first. The blushing maidal who found a red ear of corn, placed in the shock by the hostess, received a kiss from her partner. After the husking bee, homemade ice cream was turned by the young fellows as they told riddles and jokes. However, since horse-drawn equipment and bailers have eliminated the need for much of the hand work, corn husking bees, along with threshing and hay-making frolics have almost disappeared.

The Amish elders usually intermingle their entertainment with aspects of work. A classic example is the fun and frolic of a barn-raising. Here, a group of neighbors get together and build a barn from the ground up to the finished structure in one day, with a lot of hard, steady work. This is viewed as a day off from their farm duties to laugh, joke and eat with their friends and neighbors.

The elder women may get together for a rug making or a quilting. Although this is work, it is looked forward to as the non-Amish look forward to a day at the park.

An auction sale in the neighborhood is another good excuse for a day off. All work stops as they go off to the sale, whether they want to buy anything or not. The exciting atmosphere of an auction, whether it is a household sale or a cattle sale, becomes an obsession with the Amish. An extra bonus, of course, is gained if they happen onto a bargain "good and cheap." At these sales there is always an exciting game of corner ball going on, which the older Amishmen sometimes enter into.

Hobbies are another form of entertainment. Most every older person has a hobby. These may consist of wood-carving, rug making, cane furniture making, lace making, tole-painting, or some other useful craft. Those that become real good at their hobby usually place their products on sale at various fairs held in Lancaster County during the summer months.

The most favorite pastime and entertainment for the Amish is feasting and fellowship. It is seldom that a visitor to their homes is not asked to stay for a meal. The thought of communicating together and sharing problems and joys is most rewarding to the Amishman.

And the peace of God,
which passeth all understanding,
shall keep your hearts and
minds . . .

Phil. 4:7

Lo, children are an heritage of the Lord: and the fruit of the womb is his reward.

Psalms 127:3

Praise ye the Lord. Sing unto the Lord a new song and his praise in the congregation of saints.

Psalms 149:1

. . . thou hast nothing to draw with,
and the well is deep: from whence
then hast thou that living water?

John 4:11

Charity suffereth long, and is kind:
Charity envieth not:
Charity vaunteth not itself,
is not puffed up.
I Cor. 13:4

The son can do nothing of himself,
but what he seeth the Father do:
for what things soever he doeth,
these also doeth the son likewise.

John 5:19

For he shall give his angels charge over thee, to keep thee in all thy ways. They shall bear thee up in their hands, lest thou dash thy foot against a stone.

Psalms 91:11, 12

And behold, I am with thee, and
will keep thee in all places
whither thou goest, . . .

Gen. 28:15

He taketh the wise in their own craftiness: and the counsel of the froward is carried headlong.

Job 5:13

The Lord will give grace and glory
no good thing will be withheld
from them that walk uprightly.

Psalm 84:11

Courtship and Weddings

Sixteen is the magic age for Amish teenagers. When they reach this age they are given a courting buggy and a beautiful, spirited horse. They get to meet many of the opposite sex as they participate in the get-acquainted games they play at young people's gatherings and singings they attend.

Courtships are usually started by the young fellows as flirting by Amish girls is forbidden. However, if a lad finds that he is interested in a girl but is too bashful to pursue, his friends and her friends arrange to "put them together" at the next young people's gathering. Once the two start dating, the lad will usually use his open courting buggy and escort the young lady to church, singings, hoedowns, and young people's gatherings during Amish holidays. Eventually, the young fellow will take the initiative and go to the lady's house to meet her parents and become a little better acquainted. In all probability a steady courtship will begin.

When marriage takes place, it traditionally does so during the month of November, the festive month just after harvest has been completed. When November arrives, the young lady's parents will make provisions for the wedding day, which will be either on a Tuesday or a Thursday. Friends and neighbors will gather at the bride's home the day before the wedding to start preparations for the day of feasting. Scores of chickens and ducks will be slaughtered for roasting; loads of celery will be taken from the garden and cleaned; bags of potatoes will be peeled; potato chips will be fried in open iron kettles full of hot lard; dozens of cakes and pies will be baked; and many other delicious foods will be prepared.

On the day of the wedding, friends and relatives start arriving by 8 A.M. The hostler in charge parks the buggies, unhitches and waters the horses. At 8:30 the ceremony begins. Several hymns are chanted, consuming as much as thirty minutes. A minister will then preach for forty-five minutes after which a Bishop will preach the traditional wedding sermon for more than one hour. At the conclusion of this sermon, the bride and groom, who have been sitting in the center of the congregation, are summoned by the Bishop to the front, or a centrally located vantage point. A ten-minute wedding ceremony is held, after which the congregation kneels for prayer and a dismissal hymn.

The bride and groom wear no special wedding gown or tuxedo for the occasion. Their Sunday best also doubles for their wedding dress.

By the time the last hymn is completed, noon has arrived. The adults convert the backless benches into tables which are soon filled with the delicious foods prepared the day before. The guests, who may number five hundred or more, spend the rest of the day feasting and merry-making.

The bride and groom do not go on a honeymoon as we know it. As a matter of fact, they do not live together until they set up housekeeping the following spring. After the wedding, the bride and groom begin weekend visitation tours of all the adult relatives that attended the wedding. Every Friday evening, the groom will pick up his bride from her home and will make their first visit of the weekend. They will stay for the night, have breakfast the following morning, and leave. They then visit the next family where they will have lunch, chat a while and then visit a third family, where they will have supper. After supper they will leave to visit another family where they will spend the night, and have breakfast on Sunday morning. The cycle will then be repeated. On Monday morning, the groom will return the bride to her home and he will return to his until the following Friday when the visitation cycle will be repeated. During each visit the newlyweds receive gifts, called Haus-Dier, from their hosts. By springtime all is ready for the couple to set up house-keeping and start raising a large family.

The Amish concept of marriage is based on Heb. 134, wherein it says, "Marriage is honourable in all, and the bed is undefiled: but whoremongers and adulterers, God will judge." It is this exhortation that makes divorce virtually unheard of in the Amish society.

Once married, the bond between husband and wife tends to be a tie of respect rather than one of love. They seem to join together as members of a group who must personally maintain the standards and dignity of their goals rather than the personal sentiments and feelings for one another. Affection is believed to be purely a sacred and private matter not to be socialized. The family purposely ignores it, and the slightest outward display or gesture is viewed with disgust.

Each child that is born into the family is accepted as a gift from God and of His divine will; hence any form of birth control would be interfering with divine will. Large families of five to sixteen children are common and a blessing to the Amish in that it propogates their society and provides the labor needed to compete with the modern mechanized farmer.

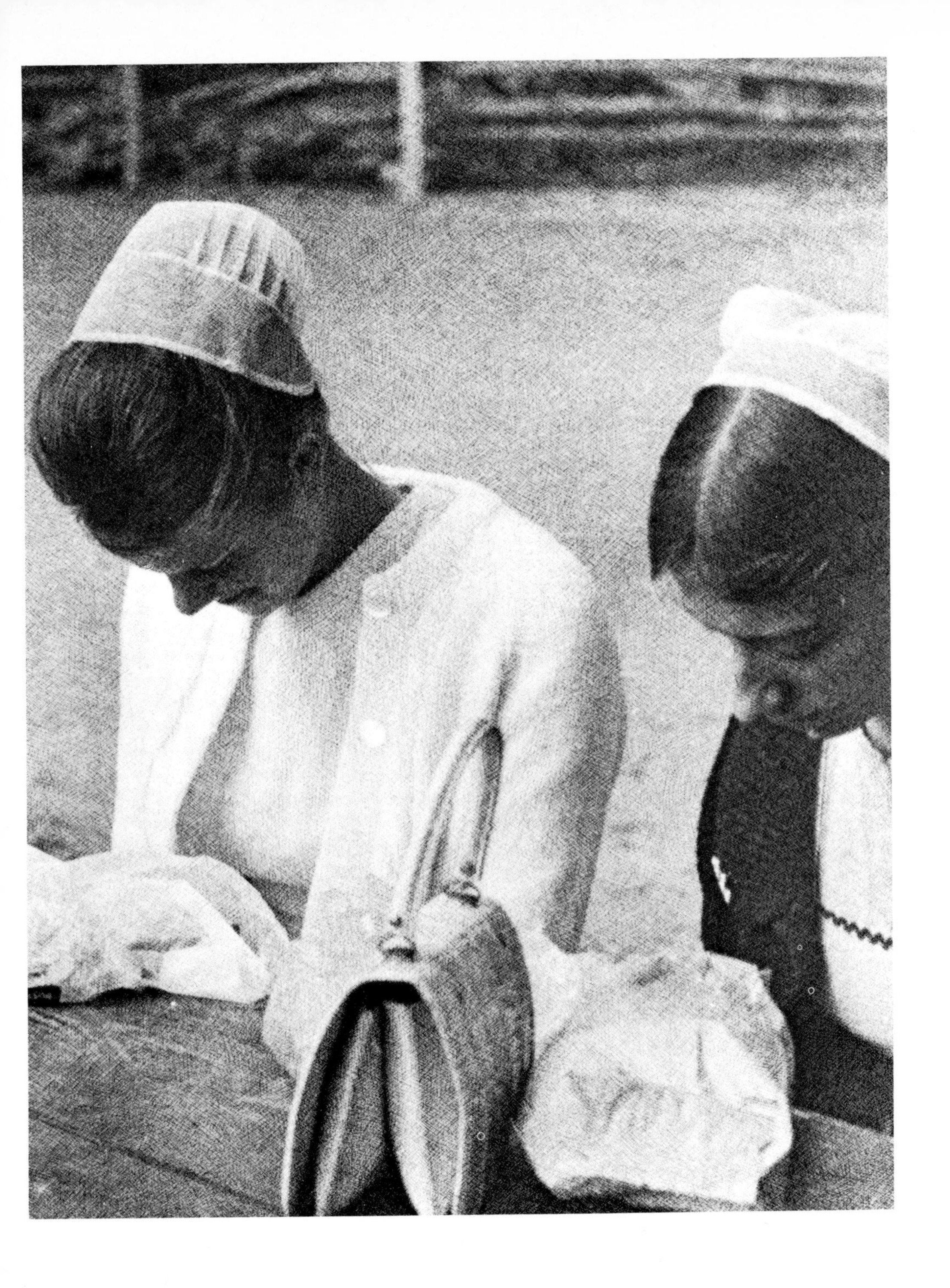

Praying always with all prayer and supplication in the Spirit . . .
Ephesians 6:18

There is no fear in love: but perfect love casteth out fear: because fear hath torment. He that feareth is not made perfect in love.

I John 4:18

Thou wilt shew me the path of life:
in thy presence is fulness of joy:
at thy right hand
there are pleasures for evermore.

Psalm 16:11

Now therefore ye are no more strangers and foreigners, but fellow citizens with the saints, and of the household of God.

Eph. 2:19

For as the rain cometh down, . . .
from heaven, and returneth not
thither, but watereth the earth,
and maketh it bring forth and
bud, that it may give seed to the
sower, and bread to the eater:

Isaiah 55:10

Strengthened with all might,
according to his glorious power,
unto all patience and longsuffering
with joyfulness.

Colo. 1:11

And be ye kind one to another,
tenderhearted, forgiving one
another . . . .

Eph. 4:32

Ordnung

(Rules for Living)

The social and religious aspects of Amish life are so closely interwoven as to be virtually inseparable. These rules for living are propagated in the Amish church service. Parental control is absolute within the family. Children are taught how to dress and how to deport themselves from the time they attain awareness. However, when Amish children enter their teen years they begin to think for themselves; and, typical of teenagers the world over, Amish children's ideas do not always coincide with those of their parents.

Elders of the sect encourage parents to make it practically mandatory that each teenager seek membership in the church during the late teen years. This membership entails special religious education instructions which are generally given from April to October. At this time all young people involved will meet with their particular Bishop and his ministers (there are usually four or five) for approximately half an hour during each church service. Detailed instructions are given on how to dress, personal deportment, and the do's and don'ts of Amish religious practice . . . such as the following:

SEPARATION FROM THE WORLD

"Love not the world, neither the things
that are in the world, If any man love
the world, the love of the Father is not in
him." I John 2:15

"and the world hated them, because they
are not of the world, even as I am not
of the world." John 17:14

"Wherefore come out from among them,
and be ye separate, saith the Lord,
and touch not the unclean thing." II Cor. 6:17

HUMILITY AND HOLINESS

"And being found in fashion as a man,
He humbled Himself, and became obedient
unto death, even the death of the cross." Phil. 2:8

". . . be ye holy, for I am holy." I Peter 1:16

HARD WORK AND FARMING

"Therefore the Lord God sent him forth
from the Garden of Eden to till the soil
from whence he was taken." Gen. 3:23

REFUSAL TO GO TO WAR

"For the weapons of our warfare are
not carnal, but mighty through God to
the pulling down of strongholds." II Cor. 10:4

". . . be gentle unto all men, apt to teach,
forbearing." II Tim. 2:24

". . . whosoever shall smite thee on thy right
cheek, turn to him the other also." Matt. 5:39

". . . if my kingdom were of this world,
then would my servants fight . . ." John 18:36

SUBMISSION TO HUSBAND

"Wives, submit yourselves unto your own
husbands, as unto the Lord.
For the husband is the head of the wife,
even as Christ is the head of the church . . ." Eph. 5:22-23

WEARING APRON OVER DRESS

". . . and they sewed fig leaves together, and
made themselves aprons." Gen. 3:7

WOMEN'S BONNETS

"But every woman that prayeth or prophesieth
with her head uncovered dishonoreth her head." I Cor. 11:5

WOMEN'S CLOTHING, NO JEWELRY

". . . that women adorn themselves in modest
apparel . . . not with plaited hair, or gold,
or pearls, or costly array." I Timothy 2:9

ABSTINENCE FROM STRONG DRINK

"Do not drink wine nor strong drink, thou,
nor thy sons with thee." Lev. 10:9

"Wine is a mocker, strong drink is raging:
and whosoever is deceived thereby is not wise." Prov. 20:1

SELF DENIAL AND ASCETIC LIFE

"And He said to them all, if any man will
come after me, let him deny himself and
take up his cross daily." Luke 9:23

FELLOWSHIP AND FEASTING

"When ye come together to eat, tarry one
for another." I Cor. 11:33

ATTITUDE AGAINST LAW

"And if any man sue thee at the law, and
take away thy coat, let him have thy cloak
also." Matt. 5:40

UNIFORMITY OF DRESS AND TRANSPORTATION
(Hair, Beard, Home, etc.)

"Endeavoring to keep the unity of the spirit
in the bond of peace." Eph. 4:3

". . . Ye are called in one body, and be ye
thankful." Col. 3:15

REFUSAL TO BUY LIFE INSURANCE

"But if any provide not for his own and especially for those of his own house, he has denied the faith and is worse than an infidel." I Tim. 5:8

LIMITED SCHOOLING

"For wisdom of the world is foolishness with God." I Cor. 3:19

CHURCH IN HOMES

"The Lord of Heaven and Earth dwelleth not in temples made with hands." Acts 17:24

SUBMISSION TO BISHOPS AND DEACONS

"Likewise, ye younger, submit yourselves unto the elders. Yea, all of you be subject one to another." I Peter 5:5

CHOOSING BISHOP BY LOT

"And they prayed, and said, Thou, Lord, which knowest the hearts of all men, show whether of these two Thou hast chosen (to take the place of Judas) . . . and they gave forth their lots and the lot fell upon Matthias . . ." Acts I:23:26

FOOT WASHING

". . . He poureth water into a basin, and began to wash the disciples' feet . . ." John 13:5

EXCOMMUNICATION AND SHUNNING

"Nevertheless, if thou warn the wicked of his way to turn from it: if he does not turn from his way, he shall die in his iniquity." Ezekiel 33:9

". . . if any man that is called a brother be a fornicator, or covetous, or an idolater, or a railer or drunkard, or an extortioner: with such a one do not eat." I Cor. 5:11

"To deliver such an one unto Satan for the destruction of the flesh." I Cor. 5:5

As and when each teenager proves capable of meeting all requirements of the church he or she becomes a member during a traditional ceremony which is held in the fall of the year. All rules and regulations are reaffirmed during this ceremony. When each new member has taken his specific vows, there follows a formal baptism by the pouring method.

All Amish adults are expected to adhere to these rules of living if they are to remain in good standing with the church. Should a member fall guilty of violating one or more of the ordinances, he or she is refused communion until such time as public repentance and confession is made before the church. If this repentance and confession is not made, excommunication will surely follow.

Horses and buggies are expected to be used for transportation. When distances involved are not practical with horse and buggy, a car with a non-Amish driver may be hired.

Since Amish families generally live on farms, agricultural equipment is involved in the ordinances. Very rigid rules govern this equipment and are strictly observed. All farm equipment must be horse-drawn or powered. Electricity may not be installed in the house or the barn, telephones may not be installed in the home, nor may modern bath or bathroom conveniences be used. Wheels on horse-drawn vehicles may not have rubber tires; this applies to farm equipment as well as buggies, carriages and wagons.

Since Amish church is held in the homes of a given district every second Sunday, the problem of off Sundays presents itself. To visit a church service of another denomination on the off Sunday, or on any other Sunday or holiday, is not tolerated. All Amish are expected to worship only with their own people and order. If the Bishop of an Amish sect knows of any offenders, disciplinary action usually follows. It is felt that fellowship with the more liberal branches of the Amish or Mennonites in their district might lead to a desire of members to become part of the liberal group . . . which could start an exodus from the Old Order Amish.

Property insurance is frowned upon by the Amish. They feel that their money would be integrated with that of non-Amish policy holders, and this would be a violation of James 1:27 . . . "Be ye not unequally yoked together with unbelievers." The Amish feel that they are their "Brothers Keepers," and when an act of God destroys the property of a devout brother, he is bearing the wrath of God for the whole community. Hence, the Amishman feels he is morally obligated to the penance of hard work in assisting the brother who has born God's wrath for him. Lightning rods are not found on Amish buildings; this, they believe, would be an attempt of little man to thwart the will of God. This same philosophy underlies the Amishmans refusal to buy life insurance. "Who are we to gamble on the life span God Almighty affords us with an insurance policy?" As the parents cared for and nurtured them in their infancy, so also should the children care for the elders in their twilight years here on earth. Are we not our brothers keeper?

Children, obey your parents in the Lord: for this is right.

Ephesians 6:1

*For thou art my lamp, O Lord:
and the Lord will lighten my
darkness.*

II Samuel 22:29

In like manner also, that women adorn themselves in modest apparel, with shamefacedness and sobriety; not with broided hair, or gold, or pearls, or costly array:

I Timothy 2:9

But every woman that prayeth or
prophesieth with her head
uncovered dishonoureth her head:
for that is even all one as if she
were shaven.

I Corinthians 11:5

Be ye therefore wise as serpents,
and harmless as doves.

Matthew 10:16

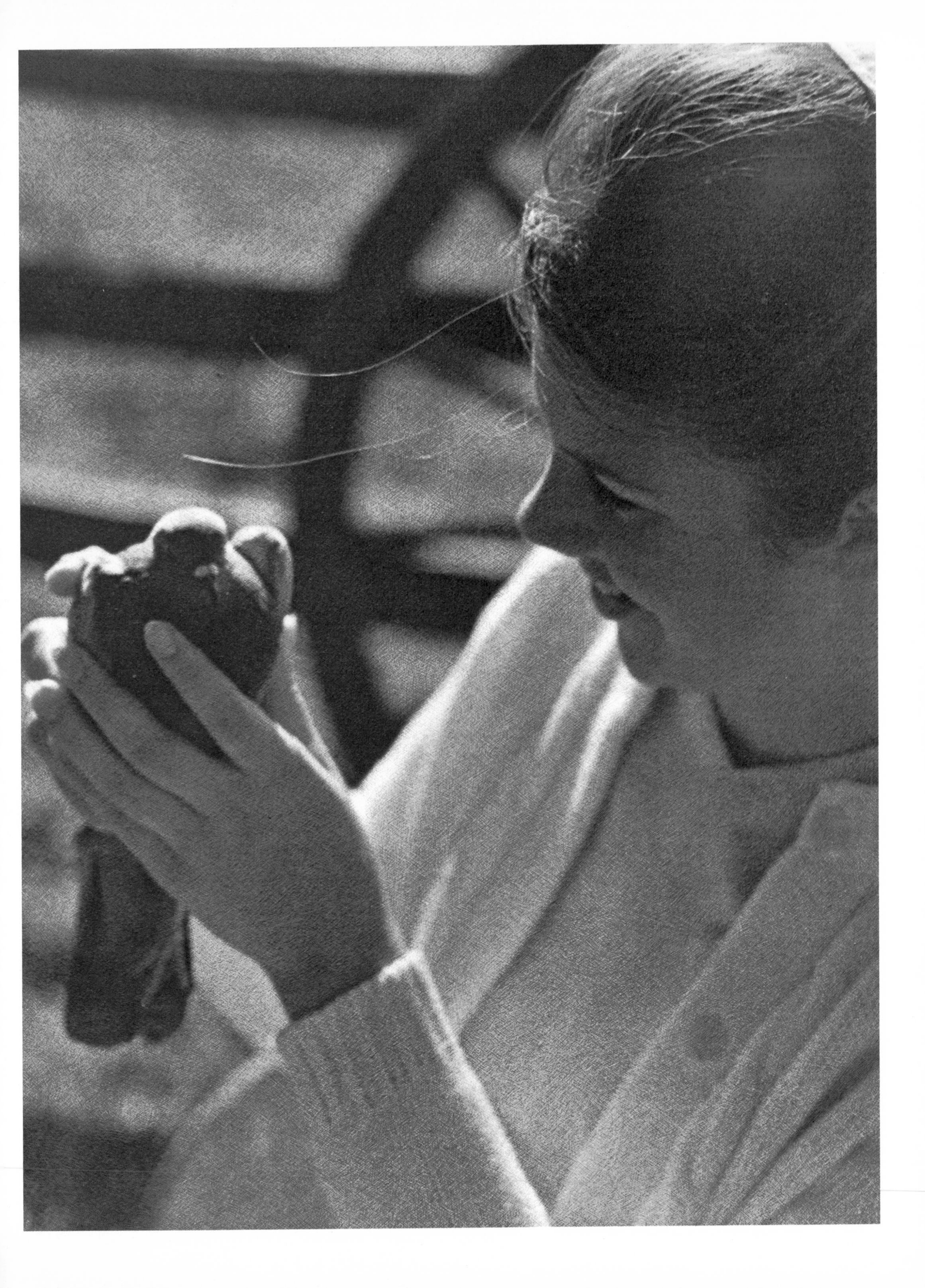

Humble yourselves in the sight of the Lord, and he shall lift you up.

James 4:10

Blessed are the meek: for they
shall inherit the earth.

Matthew 5:5

With all lowliness and meekness,
with longsuffering, forbearing one
another in love:
Endeavouring to keep the unity of
the Spirit in the bond of peace.
Eph. 4:2, 3

To everything there is a season,
and a time to every purpose under
the heaven: A time to be born,
and a time to die: a time to plant
and a time to pluck up that which
is planted:

Ecl. 3:1-2

And thine ears shall hear a word
behind thee, saying, This is the
way, walk ye in it, when ye turn
to the right hand, and when ye
turn to the left.

Isaiah 30:21

Now therefore hearken unto me,
O ye children: for blessed
are they that keep my ways.
Proverbs 8:32

Blessed Earth and Farming

The Amishman is born to work the soil. He feels that the Bible, from cover to cover, exhorts him to replenish the earth and till the soil by the sweat of his brow and to bring forth an abundant harvest. The determined soberness of his face reflects the sanctity of his purpose, not only to earn dollars, but to fulfill God's will on the land of which God has made him steward. The operation and economics of the large farm is his responsibility, while the woman is the general manager of the home and household finances. The youngsters, both boys and girls, are given responsibilities for the animals as well as a multiplicity of chores in the garden and in the field. Although the woman's responsibility is the operation of the home, during harvest time she and the older girls are in the field helping the men.

The scriptures in John 9:4 commission the Amish to work "while it is day, for the night cometh when no man can work." Thus, precious few moments of daylight escape the Amishman's eagerness to fulfill God's command.

The academic world and science are preoccupied with theory and the reconstruction of the order of nature while the Amishman is awed by the orderliness of the seasons, the heavens, the world of growing plants, and animals, and the process of living and dying. The Amish, with this philosophy, have prospered on the land more often than their English neighbors who are engulfed in the high cost of mechanization and finally forced to sell and move to industrial or more lucrative livelihoods.

Lancaster County, Pennsylvania, which has gained the distinction as the "Garden Spot of the Nation," represents an intensive kind of farming on relatively small acreage by the Amish community.

Most of the food used by the Amish family is grown, canned, butchered, or baked on the farm. An Amish pantry or cold cellar, with all the jars of fruits and vegetables, the crocks of pudding, luscious bolognas, and dried beefs hanging from the hand-hewn rafters is a sight to behold. The huge piles of potatoes, turnips, sweet potatoes and other stored foods are more than enough to last till the next harvest. The surplus is used for church affairs, hay making and threshing frolics, as well as for unexpected emergencies which may hit the members of the community, such as barn fires, deaths and floods.

Just as the Amish farmer loves the soil, the object of his labor, so also does he love his animals and farm equipment. After a hard day's work, the mules and horses are fed and bedded down, and the implements and the simplest pieces of machinery are greased and put away.

While the non-Amish neighbor rushes through his work with a variety of power equipment, the Amish plod on methodically with animal and human power. Some very basic mechanization is sanctioned to power small equipment. A common sight along small streams are creaking water wheels which supply power, by long cables, to pump handles at the barn. This provides constant spurts of water for the home and the livestock. Windmills are also used to supply power in case of water wheel drought.

The horse and goat treadmills have been replaced by the noisy one-cylinder gas engine which is portable and is used for milk coolers, corn shelling, washing machines, and ice cream and butter churns.

Another acceptable source of power is the massive old steam engine. This power source is not to be used in tilling the soil, but for belt power in threshing and in filling the silo. It is also used in steaming of tobacco beds to kill insects and purify the ground before tobacco seeds are planted. The dramatic hissing and puffing of the engine, as clouds of smoke billow from its stack, thrills the Amishman as he shovels more coal into the boiler. A gentle pull on the whistle cord brings a shrill two-tone blast, and also a smile on the face of the most stern-faced Amishman.

All other conveyances rely solely on horse power. Horses are divided into three classes: the driving horse, work horse, and draft mule.

Driving horses are used to pull the buggies and carts, and will usually serve their owners ten to fifteen years if properly cared for. Young Amish boys seek out the youngest, most spirited horses for their buggies, to impress the Amish girls they will date. Sometimes disqualified race horses are bought and used for this purpose.

The work horses, usually heavy Belgium or Clydesdale, have a life span of from twenty to thirty years, and may weigh from one to two thousand pounds. These are used for the heavy farm work.

The draft mule, which is a cross between a donkey and a horse, gives a longer work day with less feed and water. Thus they are more desirable and therefore, harder to acquire.

Because of the concentrated use of horses and horse drawn wagons, the nostalgic village blacksmith, who was part of early America, is still spotted throughout Lancaster County. An Amish horse needs to be shod every three or four months, depending on how much he is driven on the macadam roads.

Most of the blacksmiths are farriers specializing in horseshoeing, and do not make wagons. However, Amish carriage shops still in existence are booked one year in advance with Amish wagon orders.

. . . as unto a light that
shineth in a dark place,
until the day dawn, and the
day star arise in your hearts.
II Peter 1:19

The land shall not be sold forever;
for the land is mine; for ye are
strangers and sojourners with me.

Leviticus 25:23

No man, having put his hand to
the plough, and looking back, is
fit for the kingdom of God.

Luke 9:62

But my God shall supply all your need according to his riches in glory by Christ Jesus.

Phil. 4:19

The earth is the Lord's and the fulness thereof; the world, and they that dwell therein.

Psalms 24:1

Blessed is the man that walketh
not in the counsel
of the ungodly, . . .

Psalm 1:1

He which soweth sparingly shall
reap also sparingly; and he which
soweth bountifully shall reap
also bountifully.

II Corinthians 10:6

In the sweat of thy face shalt thou eat bread, till thou return unto the ground; for out of it wast thou taken: for dust thou art, and unto dust shalt thou return.

Genesis 3:19

As newborn babes, desire the sincere milk of the word, that ye may grow thereby.

I Peter 2:2

He that observeth the wind shall
not sow; and he that regardeth the
clouds shall not reap.

Ecclesiastes 11:4

. . ., and he that smootheth with
the hammer him that smote the
anvil, saying, It is ready for the
soldering: and he fastened it with
nails, that it should not be moved.

Isaiah 41:7

Therefore thus saith the Lord God unto them: Behold I, even I, will judge between the fat cattle and between the lean cattle.

Ezekiel 34:20

Thou shalt call, and I will answer thee: thou wilt have a desire to the work of thine hands.

Job 14:15

. . . although the fields shall yield
no meat: the flock shall be cut
off from the fold, and there shall
be no herd in the stalls:

Yet I will rejoice in the Lord . . .

Habakkuk 3:17, 18

Man goeth forth unto his work
and to his labour until the evening.

Psalm 104:23

I must work the works of him that sent me, while it is day: the night cometh, when no man can work.

John 9:4

I have made the earth,
and created man upon it:
I, even my hands, have stretched
out the heavens, and all their host
have I commanded.
Isaiah 45:12

Honour thy father and thy mother: that thy days may be long upon the land which the Lord thy God giveth thee.
Exodus 20:12

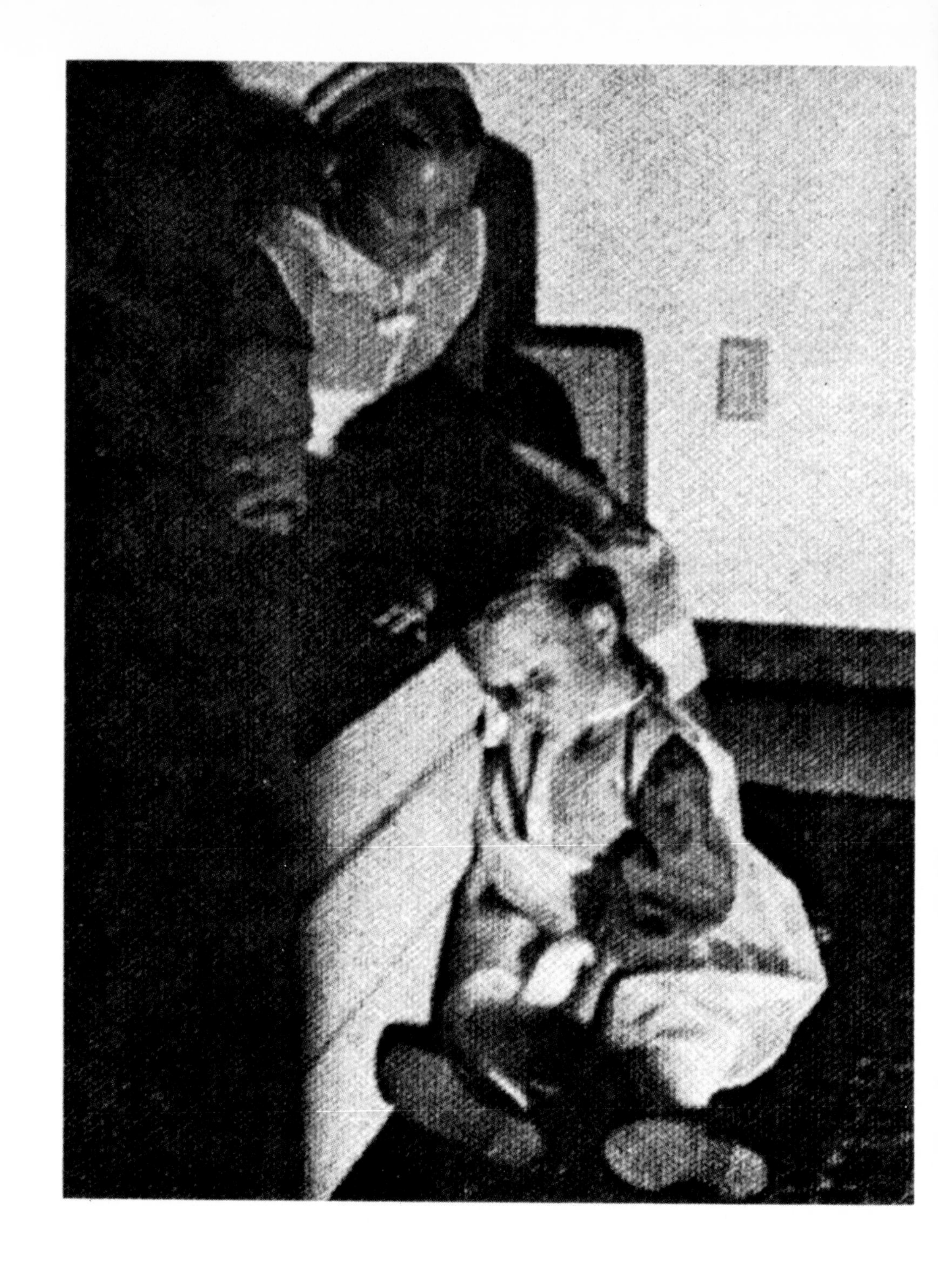

And be ye kind one to another, tenderhearted, forgiving one another . . . .
Eph. 4:32

In his humiliation his judgment was taken away: and who shall declare his generation? for his life is taken from the earth.
Acts 8:33

And the fruit of righteousness
is sown in peace of them
that make peace.
James 3:18

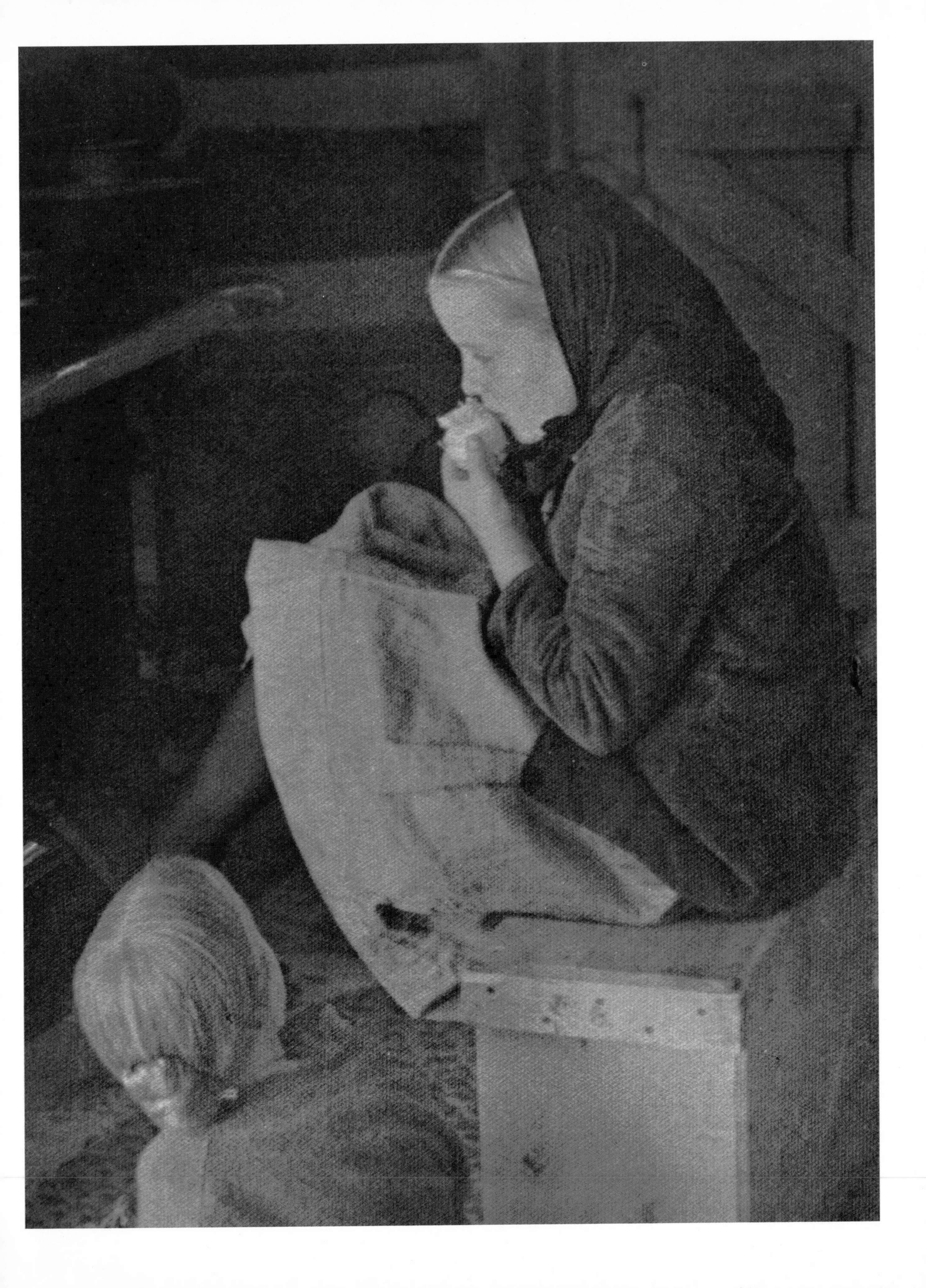

Teach me thy way, O Lord,
and lead me in a plain path,
because of mine enemies.
Psalms 27:11

"But let patience have her perfect work, that ye may be perfect and entire, wanting nothing."

James 1:4

"We came unto the land whither
thou sentest us, and surely it
floweth with milk and honey:
and this is the fruit of it."

Numbers 13:26

"She looketh well to the ways of her household, and eateth not the bread of idleness."

Proverbs 31:27

"Therefore if thine enemy hunger,
feed him: if he thirst,
give him drink: . . . . .
Be not overcome of evil, but
overcome evil with good."

Romans 12: 20, 21

*"For now we see through a glass,
darkly: but then face to face: now I
know in part: but then shall I know even as
also I am known."*

I Corinthians 13:12

"Peace I leave with you, my peace I give unto you: not as the world giveth, give I unto you. Let not your heart be troubled, neither let it be afraid."

John 14:27